M000210298

Thirsty For God

By Mark Hart
Something More Series Editor

I was out on my run one hot summer morning in Arizona. A mile in, I realized I'd forgotten my water bottle. "No problem," I thought to myself. "I've done this run a hundred times. I'll be fine." Sadly, my pride-ridden brain forgot to inform my dehydrated body. By the time I turned the corner for mile number three, my legs began to lock up. I became dizzy and nauseated, and at one point, I'm certain the grim reaper was running beside me. Even my guardian angel was asking for a drink!

I made the mistake of thinking I could survive on my own—I didn't need anything or anyone else. I was wrong. The proverb was correct: "Pride does (indeed) go before folly" (cf. Proverbs 16:18). And I've made similar mistakes in my Christian journey. The key to avoiding dehydration—physical or spiritual—is to have and drink water *before* you actually thirst.

Are You Thriving or Just Surviving?

We know our bodies were created with needs. But so were our souls. Creation is designed to need not just creation but the Creator. The One who breathes life into us loves us enough to design us with spiritual needs as well. We have not only a desire for the lifeblood of earth (food and water) but also for the lifeblood of heaven in prayer and sacrament. The question is this: do we want to merely survive or truly live?

In the famous encounter between Jesus and the Samaritan woman at the well (John 4:4-42), the woman may have gone

Getting More Out of Prayer

SOMETHING MORE FAITH SERIES

By Patricia Mitchell

Mark Hart, Series Editor

Published by The Word Among Us Press
7115 Guilford Drive, Suite 100
Frederick, Maryland 21704

22 21 20 19 18   1 2 3 4 5

ISBN: 978-1-59325-326-4

Nihil Obstat: The Reverend Michael Morgan, J.D., J.C.L.
                 Censor Librorum
                 November 8, 2017

Imprimatur: +Most Reverend Felipe J. Estévez, S.T.D
                 Bishop of St. Augustine
                 November 8, 2017

Cover and text design by Suzanne Earl

Made and printed in the United States of America

seeking water, but it was the Living Water—Jesus Christ—who approached asking for a drink. She, like many of us, had been in survival mode: spiritually dehydrated and used to it. It was not until she encountered the Lord that she began to comprehend the difference between surviving and thriving. As the *Catechism of the Catholic Church* reminds us,

> Jesus thirsts; his asking arises from the depths of God's desire for us. Whether we realize it or not, prayer is the encounter of God's thirst with ours. God thirsts that we may thirst for him. (2560)

The reality is that even when we pray, even when we put forth the effort, it is really still God pursuing us. Prayer is where earth and heaven collide. Prayer is where our earthly thirst is temporarily satiated by a heavenly spring. It is in prayer that light breathes into moments of darkness, hope vanquishes fear, peace shatters anxiety, and healing pours into every wound. Prayer does not eliminate our crosses, but it offers us a new perspective on them. Prayer is where the cross changes shoulders.

The Power of Proactive Prayer

The more we pray, the more we will desire to do so. The sooner we realize the power of proactive prayer in the every day, rather than "reactive" prayer in times of desperation, the more we will trust in the love and presence of God in our daily lives. We soon begin to see that prayer does not "help" our relationship with God; prayer *is* our relationship with God.

Any relationship, however, takes time and work; a relationship with God is no different. God is willing to fulfill his end. The Lord bids us to ask, seek, and knock (Matthew 7:7). Note that all three of those actions require *effort* on our part. That being said, he promises us that "when you . . . pray to me, I will listen to you" (Jeremiah 29:12), and we are reminded, "Draw near to God, and he will draw near to you" (James 4:8).

In the pages that follow, you'll be given simple and practical ways to encounter God profoundly and daily. In the included reflection questions and action steps, you'll come face-to-face again (or possibly for the first time ever) with a God who not only looks at you with great love, just as you are, but who wants you to know him as a trustworthy and faithful friend.

St. Augustine said we are all beggars before God. As such, humility really is the foundation of all prayer (CCC, 2559). Your openness to this booklet and the exercises suggested demonstrate humility on your part. The Holy Spirit wants to reward your act of openness. God will not be outdone in generosity.

So before you turn this page and venture into the unknown encounter God has in store for you, say a quick prayer. Give the Lord permission to speak to you in a new way. Ask the Lord to come dwell in you in new ways. Ask the Lord to illuminate your mind. Invite the Lord to occupy your heart. Invite the Lord to move in your soul . . . in his time and according to his perfect plan.

Pray, "*Come, Holy Spirit.*" Repeat the phrase several times before you move on to Session 1. The Lord is waiting for you. He is the Living Water, ready to satisfy your deepest thirst.

How To Use This Booklet

Whether used individually or in a small group, each session of *Getting More Out of Prayer* is designed to take less than an hour. If you are using it on your own, remember to begin and end each session with prayer. You might also want to find someone to talk to about what you've learned. If you are part of a small group, the following guidelines can help you have a successful, fruitful experience.

1. Establish a prayerful environment by taking the time to pray before beginning. Ask the Holy Spirit to be with your group. Pray, "Come, Holy Spirit" slowly. Allow for a few moments of silence. Then say a prayer together, like the Our Father, a Hail Mary, or a Glory Be.

2. Have one or two people read the Scripture passage aloud that appears at the beginning of each session.

3. Assume everyone has read the commentary beforehand. The group facilitator could ask everyone if this is the case. If not, you might ask one or two people to try to summarize the main points of the commentary, or say what most struck them from reading it.

4. Begin discussing the questions, being careful not to rush to the next question, especially if not everyone has spoken. Some people need more time to gather their thoughts. People who tend to be quiet may need a moment of silence before they feel free to express themselves.

5. Try to bring the discussion back to the questions or text if it strays. Any member of the group should feel free to gently steer the discussion to the next point.

6. When you are finished with the questions, the group facilitator should outline the prayer exercises presented and ask whether anyone has a question about them. Encourage participants to use these prayer exercises between sessions.

7. End with prayer. Perhaps someone could pray spontaneously, thanking God for the opportunity to gather together to pray and study God's word.

8. Make sure you know when and where you are gathering for the next session. Encourage participants to read the Scripture passage and commentary and to reflect on the questions for the next session before the group gathers again. This will help them get the most out of each session.

For more suggestions for small groups, go online to wau.org/faithseries.

A Gaze of Love

Luke 19:1-10

¹[Jesus] came to Jericho and intended to pass through the town. ²Now a man there named Zacchaeus, who was a chief tax collector and also a wealthy man, ³was seeking to see who Jesus was; but he could not see him because of the crowd, for he was short in stature. ⁴So he ran ahead and climbed a sycamore tree in order to see Jesus, who was about to pass that way. ⁵When he reached the place, Jesus looked up and said to him, "Zacchaeus, come down quickly, for today I must stay at your house." ⁶And he came down quickly and received him with joy. ⁷When they all saw this, they began to grumble, saying, "He has gone to stay at the house of a sinner." ⁸But Zacchaeus stood there and said to the Lord, "Behold, half of my possessions, Lord, I shall give to the poor, and if I have extorted anything from anyone I shall repay it four times over." ⁹And Jesus said to him, "Today salvation has come to this house because this man too is a descendant of Abraham. ¹⁰For the Son of Man has come to seek and to save what was lost."

Zacchaeus was a busy man. As chief tax collector, he had to make sure that all the citizens of Jericho were paying what they owed the Roman government. He was also a rich man, overcharging his fellow Jews so that he could retain some of the money for himself. And yet sinner though he was, he had heard about Jesus traveling through his city and wanted to catch a glimpse of this holy man. Knowing that he might be mocked for doing so, he climbed the sycamore tree anyway so that he could see above the crowds.

Something amazing happened in those few seconds when Jesus passed by—a look that changed Zacchaeus' heart and made him respond eagerly to Jesus' offer to come to his home. What was it about that look that made such a difference in Zacchaeus' life?

A Change of Heart

Like Zacchaeus, we are all sinners—we have all done things we are not proud of. And yet Jesus looks at us in the same way he looked at Zacchaeus. He sees not our sin but our potential; he sees us with eyes of love. That gaze can melt our hearts and cause us to respond as Zacchaeus did, with immediacy, exuberance, and expectation.

Have you ever allowed Jesus to look at you as he looked at Zacchaeus? We often think of what we must do for God. We must obey the commandments, love our neighbor, and fulfill our religious obligations. All well and good. But often we skip the crucial first step. We must allow Jesus to look at us with love.

How can we receive the love of Jesus? By sitting at his feet in prayer. It is there that Jesus wants to lavish his love on us. And like Zacchaeus, if we are eager to climb that tree, we will put ourselves in a place where we can experience God's love.

We might be tempted to view prayer as another religious obligation, another demand that God makes on us. We may feel guilty that we aren't praying enough, or that we go to God only when we need help from him. Of course, he is always happy to hear from us, even when it's only a five-second plea for help. But God desires so much more.

We must allow Jesus to look at us with love.

Do you desire more as well? We hope the next five sessions can help you to draw closer to Jesus so that you can receive the love he wants to give you. That experience—of being known and loved more than you ever have before—will draw you to him again and again. Prayer will become no longer an obligation but something you desire, something you would not want to miss each and every day of your life.

Questions for Reflection and Discussion

1. Why do you think Zacchaeus made such an effort to see Jesus? What might he have been thinking as he made the decision to go and see him? To climb the tree?

2. Jesus saw a "descendant of Abraham" (literally, "a son of Abraham") when he looked at Zacchaeus. What do you think Jesus sees when he gazes at you? How might he describe you?

3. Why do you think Jesus immediately invited himself to Zacchaeus' house? In what ways is he inviting himself to your "home"? Have you accepted his invitation?

4. What comes to mind when you think about prayer? How would you describe it? How would you describe your own prayer?

5. Have you ever felt Jesus' gaze of love? What was that like? If not, what may have prevented you?

This week make it a point to spend some time with Jesus in prayer. Find a quiet place where you won't be disturbed. Maybe you could visit your parish church or a local chapel, or find a quiet bench at a park where you won't be distracted.

Try to quiet your mind by taking some deep breaths. Let go of your worries and concerns. You can talk to Jesus about your needs at some other time, but during this time of prayer, just allow the Lord to gaze at you.

Begin your prayer by asking the Holy Spirit to open your heart to Jesus. Be open to the love of God, even if you feel unworthy or unlovable. Be still and receive the love of Jesus, even if you think that's not enough and that you should instead be *doing* something for God instead of just *receiving* something from him.

Read the Scripture passage about Zacchaeus again, and imagine that you are Zacchaeus and that you have climbed that sycamore tree. Instead of looking for Jesus, however, allow him to find you. Imagine he is looking for you among the crowd because he loves you and wants you to know how much you mean to him. He is singling you out! What would his eyes look like as they meet yours? Would he smile at you? Would you feel his affirmation of who you are and were created to be? How would you respond?

Try this exercise several times with Luke 19 as well as with the other Gospel stories listed here.

- **The Call of Matthew (Matthew 9:9-13).** Matthew saw Jesus looking at him in a way that made him give up his former way of life. Imagine you are Matthew at your customs post. Jesus passes by and looks at you and then says, "Follow me." Imagine Jesus' face, looking at you in the same way as he must have looked at Matthew.

- **The Rich Young Man (Mark 10:17-31).** Imagine you are the rich young man and that Jesus is looking on you with love (cf. verse 21). How would you respond?

That Still Small Voice

1 Kings 19:9-13

9[The prophet Elijah] came to a cave, where he took shelter. But the word of the LORD came to him: Why are you here, Elijah? 10He answered: "I have been most zealous for the LORD, the God of hosts, but the Israelites have forsaken your covenant. They have destroyed your altars and murdered your prophets by the sword. I alone remain, and they seek to take my life." 11Then the LORD said: Go out and stand on the mountain before the LORD; the LORD will pass by. There was a strong and violent wind rending the mountains and crushing rocks before the LORD—but the LORD was not in the wind; after the wind, an earthquake—but the LORD was not in the earthquake; 12after the earthquake, fire—but the LORD was not in the fire; after the fire, a light silent sound.

13When he heard this, Elijah hid his face in his cloak and went out and stood at the entrance of the cave.

The prophet Elijah is dejected and afraid. Queen Jezebel, the pagan wife of Israel's King Ahab and a worshipper of the god Baal, intends to kill Elijah for destroying all of Baal's prophets. So he flees, leaving northern Israel and journeying to the southern city of Beersheba.

After walking forty days and forty nights, Elijah enters a cave, and when God asks him why he is there, he complains about his situation. The Lord instructs Elijah to wait for him to pass by.

Through wind, earthquake, and fire, Elijah does not hear the Lord. But when the prophet perceives "a light silent sound" (in other translations, "a still small voice"), he knows it is the Lord. Then God gives him specific instructions for succession plans for both the king and Elijah himself. (Read the rest of 1 Kings 19 if you want to see what happens next.)

The "Earthquakes" and "Fires" in Our Lives

Are you able to distinguish God's voice from the "noises" in your life? Perhaps through years of experience, Elijah knew when the Lord was "passing by." But we may miss him because we are preoccupied with the "earthquakes," "fires," and "windstorms" in our lives—our worries, trials, concerns, and even our general busyness, all of which can prevent us from hearing God. Or perhaps the myriad forms of entertainment and media we have at our fingertips 24/7 end up distracting us, drowning out God's still small voice.

God speaks to us in the silence of our hearts. The challenge we face is to quiet our minds and hearts as well as our surroundings. The best way we can begin to do that is by setting aside time each day dedicated solely to the Lord.

Finding fifteen to twenty minutes each day to pray can seem like an insurmountable challenge. But our Father is inviting us to spend time with him. If we accept that invitation, he will help us to do it.

Many people find early mornings the best time to pray. That's because the later it gets, the greater the likelihood that the demands of the day will begin to press upon us. In addition, at that time of day, our bodies are rested and (for most of us) our minds are clear. However, if you are a night owl and not a morning person, try setting aside time for prayer before you go to bed. The time of day matters less than keeping the commitment to pray daily.

> Are you able to distinguish God's voice from the "noises" in your life?

Once you've settled upon the time of day, create a special prayer corner. Find a comfortable chair, and keep your Bible nearby or a favorite spiritual book. A crucifix, an icon or other image, or a lighted candle can help to create an atmosphere for silent reflection and prayer.

Begin by taking some deep breaths and clearing your mind of any worries or concerns. As you did last week, ask the Holy Spirit to be with you, and then place yourself in God's presence.

Make the Commitment

There are many ways to pray, especially with Scripture, which will be addressed in a later session. The point here is to make the initial commitment to pray and to make it the most important priority of your day—and of your life! We can't hear God's still small voice unless we quiet ourselves and set ourselves apart (the meaning of "holiness" is "set apart for God"). God wants your friendship, but you can't be a friend to someone unless you spend time with that person.

Don't be discouraged if you aren't able at first to set aside time for prayer. Just keep trying! Maybe you need to go to bed a bit earlier and set your alarm fifteen minutes ahead of your usual wake-up time. Maybe you need to try a different time of day, or a different setting. Maybe you can start with just ten minutes, or even five. Just keep asking the Holy Spirit to inspire you—both with the desire to pray and with ideas for how to make it happen.

Questions for Reflection and Discussion

1. Why do you think God wanted Elijah to hear him in the silence? What lesson do you think Elijah learned?

2. How comfortable are you with silence? For example, are you able to ride in the car without the radio on or music playing? Are you able to be with someone when there are periods of silence?

3. How do the noise and distractions of your daily life affect you? Do you ever find time to be alone by yourself or with God?

4. How successful have you ever been in setting aside time to pray in the morning or at some point during the day? What are some obstacles you face that might prevent you from doing so?

5. Do you believe that you can hear God speaking to you in prayer? Do you recall an instance in your life in which you got a sense about something from the Lord, whether during prayer or at some other time?

Before the Next Session . . .

See how many days this week you can set aside special time for God. Before you begin, you might even want to set your timer for fifteen or twenty minutes, just to make sure you have enough time to quiet your mind and relax with the Lord.

After finding a comfortable, quiet spot to pray, try beginning your time of prayer with praise and thanksgiving.

Thank your heavenly Father for your faith and for giving you this special time with him. Praise him for sending his Son to die on the cross so that you may live. Thank him for sending his Holy Spirit to inspire and guide you.

You might then want to meditate on one of the Scripture passages below or one of your own choosing—perhaps the Gospel reading for Mass that day. Perhaps a word or phrase from that passage will strike you. Reflect on it.

Then sit quietly with God. Say, "Speak, Lord; your servant is listening." Allow yourself to be comfortable with the silence. Perhaps you will get a sense of something the Lord wants to tell you. If so, write it down. God may want to reassure you of his love or forgiveness. However, whether or not you "hear" from the Lord is not as impor tant as just sitting with him, allowing him to fill you with his love. When we intentionally open our hearts and minds to the Lord, he will fill us with whatever we need that day!

Here are some Scripture passages you can meditate on this week about listening to and hearing from God:

- **The Lord Calls Samuel (1 Samuel 3:1-11).** Imagine that you are Samuel, and that the Lord is calling your name. How do you respond?

- **The Baptism of Jesus (Matthew 3:13-17; see also Luke 3:21-22 and Mark 1:9-11).** You are a son or daughter of our heavenly Father. Imagine God saying to you the same words he spoke to Jesus: "This is my beloved Son, with whom I am well pleased."

- **The Transfiguration (Matthew 17:1-13; see also Luke 9:28-36; Mark 9:2-13).** Reflect on what it means to "listen" to God.

John 8:2-11

²Early in the morning he arrived again in the temple area, and all the people started coming to him, and he sat down and taught them. ³Then the scribes and the Pharisees brought a woman who had been caught in adultery and made her stand in the middle. ⁴They said to him, "Teacher, this woman was caught in the very act of committing adultery. ⁵Now in the law, Moses commanded us to stone such women. So what do you say?" ⁶They said this to test him, so that they could have some charge to bring against him. Jesus bent down and began to write on the ground with his finger. ⁷But when they continued asking him, he straightened up and said to them, "Let the one among you who is without sin be the first to throw a stone at her." ⁸Again he bent down and wrote on the ground. ⁹And in response, they went away one by one, beginning with the elders. So he was left alone with the woman before him. ¹⁰Then Jesus straightened up and said to her, "Woman, where are they? Has no one condemned you?" ¹¹She replied, "No one, sir." Then Jesus said, "Neither do I condemn you. Go, [and] from now on do not sin any more."

How well do you know Jesus? Do you consider him your friend?

We get to know someone well only by spending time with that person. We come to know who they are—what they enjoy, what they believe, what is important to them, what moves them, what excites them. Knowing someone well lays the groundwork for love. We can truly love someone only when we know who they are, deep down, on more than a surface level.

Do you believe that Jesus wants a deep and abiding friendship with you? He does—that's why he died on the cross for you. He wants you to know him intimately, just as he knows you intimately. How can we come to know Jesus in a deeper way? Through studying and praying with the Gospel stories.

This story of Jesus and the woman caught in adultery tells us so much about who Jesus is. When tested by the scribes and Pharisees, he does not confront them directly. Instead, he reminds them that they, too, have sinned. Then he addresses the woman. How surprised she must have been by his words to her! He does not condemn her but forgives her. He shows through his actions that he really means what he says: "I did not come to condemn the world but to save the world" (John 12:47) and "I have not come to call the righteous to repentance but sinners" (Luke 5:32).

A Heart of Mercy

Jesus has a heart of mercy; he is always ready to forgive us when we come to him in sorrow for our sins. He isn't surprised or scandalized by what we have done. Instead, he loves us and wants to set us free.

That's why he came to earth; that's why he died for us. Through his cross and resurrection, he has conquered both sin and death.

We are all aware of our sins and shortcomings and the ways in which we have fallen short of loving others. That awareness can sometimes makes us feel unworthy of Jesus' love and friendship. But this story of the woman caught in adultery—and many others in the Gospels—reminds us that we are all welcomed by Jesus, no matter what our sin or failures.

Do you believe that Jesus wants a deep and abiding friendship with you?

Our Father is inviting us to get to know our Savior and Redeemer. Through his resurrection, Jesus is alive—in his word, in the Eucharist, and in our lives. We should not be afraid to call him our friend. And we can deepen our friendship with him every day by meditating on his words and actions. The more we get to know Jesus, the more we will fall in love with him and the more he will become a real presence in our lives.

This is an invitation too good to pass up! Friendship with Jesus is life changing. We will all sin; we will all have trials and difficult times in our lives. But we don't have to travel alone. Jesus can be our companion, each and every minute of each and every day, as he will be one day in heaven.

1. What strikes you about the story of the woman caught in adultery? With whom do you most identify, the Pharisees or the woman?

2. What personal qualities does Jesus exhibit in this passage? How would you describe him to someone, based on what you see here?

3. Who is your best friend? How would you describe that friendship? In what ways does your friendship with Jesus resemble that friendship?

4. How might feelings of unworthiness keep you from drawing closer to Jesus in friendship? What else might be preventing you from deepening your friendship with Jesus?

5. Friends support each other. As a friend of Jesus, you may be called to do something for him. Are you ready to respond to that call? How might you prepare yourself?

Before the Next Session . . .

Before he ascended into heaven, Jesus promised to send the Holy Spirit to his disciples to empower them to preach the gospel (Luke 24:49; Acts 1:8). We received the Holy Spirit in Baptism and were strengthened by him in Confirmation. As St. Paul wrote, when we don't know how to pray, the Spirit prays in us (Romans 8:26-27). *The Holy Spirit is the key to fruitful prayer.* We need to rely on him to help us pray and draw closer to Jesus.

This week in prayer, begin your time with the Lord by calling on the Holy Spirit. You could pray, "Come, Holy Spirit," several times slowly. Ask him to fill you with the desire to pray, read Scripture, and get to know Jesus in a deeper way.

The following Scripture passages may be familiar to you, but we can never exhaust the riches of these stories. Choose one or find one you especially love. Read each passage over slowly several times, and then reflect on what it tells you about Jesus. What qualities do you see in him? What was his motivation for acting as he did? How did he fulfill the mission that his Father had given him? Perhaps you can make a list of these qualities in a prayer journal or talk it over with someone who is also seeking to grow in friendship with Christ.

- Jesus' Temptation in the Desert (Luke 4:1-13)
- The Cleansing of Leper (Mark 1:40-45)
- Jesus Heals a Paralyzed Man (Mark 2:3-12)
- The Healing of a Centurion's Servant (Matthew 8:5-13)
- Jesus Heals Jairus' Daughter and a Woman with a Hemorrhage (Mark 5:22-43)
- The Calming of a Storm at Sea (Mark 4:35-41)
- The Healing of Bartimaeus (Mark 10:46-52)
- The Call of Simon (Luke 5:1-11)
- The Raising of the Widow's Son (Luke 7:11-17)
- The Lament over Jerusalem (Luke 13:34-35)
- Jesus Cures a Man with a Demon (Mark 1:21-28)
- The Wedding at Cana (John 2:1-11)
- The Samaritan Woman at the Well (John 4:1-42)
- Jesus Feeds the Five Thousand (Mark 6:30-44)
- The Raising of Lazarus (John 11:1-44)
- A Woman Anoints Jesus (Luke 7:36-50)
- Jesus Cures a Woman Who Is Crippled (Luke 13:10-17)
- Jesus Clears the Temple (Matthew 21:12-17)
- The Parable of the Prodigal Son (Luke 15:11-32)
- The Parable of the Tenants (Luke 20:9-19)

In addition, the passion and resurrection narratives of each of the Gospels offer many opportunities for rich prayer, especially during Holy Week and Easter.

- Matthew 26:41–28:20
- Mark 14–16
- Luke 22:39–24:53
- John 18–21

FOUR

Freedom with the Lord

Psalm 43

¹Grant me justice, O God;
   defend me from a faithless people;
   from the deceitful and unjust rescue me.
²You, O God, are my strength.
   Why then do you spurn me?
Why must I go about mourning,
   with the enemy oppressing me?
³Send your light and your fidelity,
   that they may be my guide;
Let them bring me to your holy mountain,
   to the place of your dwelling,
⁴That I may come to the altar of God,
   to God, my joy, my delight.
Then I will praise you with the harp,
   O God, my God.
⁵Why are you downcast, my soul?
   Why do you groan within me?
Wait for God, for I shall again praise him,
   my savior and my God.

True friendship means we can be ourselves with another person. We aren't afraid to express our real feelings and concerns. With those we are close to, we don't have to put on a happy face if we are not feeling that way. We can tell our friends what is really going on. We can be authentic, transparent, and vulnerable.

The Lord wants that kind of friendship with us. He wants us to share our lives with him, just as he wants to share his life with us. So even when we are feeling sad, angry, dejected, or disappointed, he wants us to come to him and express those feelings. We may even be angry or upset with *him* because he hasn't answered our prayers in the way we want. Yet just like the psalmist, we should feel free to come to the Lord with our burdens, our complaints, and our disappointments—as well as our gratitude and joy.

We can find an outlet for expressing ourselves in the Book of Psalms, no matter what emotions we are experiencing. Among the 150 psalms are prayers of lament, thanksgiving, praise, repentance, and petition. These ancient prayers are a treasured part of the Church's liturgy. In addition to the responsorial psalm that is included in the daily Mass readings, the psalms are prayed or chanted throughout each day during the Church's Liturgy of the Hours.

In Psalm 43, the psalmist is crying out to God. He is living near Israel's northern border, far from Jerusalem, and he longs for God's presence in the Temple. God seems absent and far away, but the psalmist still ends on a hopeful note—if he is patient and waits, he will one day be able to praise the Lord in his "holy mountain."

Jesus Knows What We Feel

Though he was God, Jesus was also a human being who experienced all the emotions and challenges that we do. He was angry with the Pharisees (Matthew 23:13-33); he rejoiced when the seventy-two disciples returned from their mission trip (Luke 10:21); he felt abandoned by his Father on the cross (Matthew 27:46). So he understands what we are experiencing. And because he loves us, he wants us to come to him, daily, to share our lives with him. This includes sharing not only our joys and successes but also our sorrows and failures. He wants *all* of us—not just our "good" parts.

> In order to deepen our friendship with the Lord, we have to be real with him.

In order to deepen our friendship with the Lord, we have to be real with him. And then after we unburden ourselves, we need to listen. Perhaps he has a word of comfort or encouragement, or even an insight into a situation or a reason we should come to him for forgiveness. He can bring us to a place of acceptance, or help us to have hope that he is bringing good even out of a difficult or tragic situation.

Jesus prayed Psalm 22 on the cross when he said, "My God, my God, why have you abandoned me?" (verse 2). Yet this psalm ends with an expression of trust that the Lord will deliver his people (verses 28-32). Like the psalmist, we can end our time of prayer with praise and thanksgiving for a God who will never leave us or forsake us (Hebrews 13:5), who will be with us always, "until the end of the age" (Matthew 28:20).

Questions for Reflection and Discussion

1. The psalmist writes that God is his strength but then asks the Lord why he is being spurned (verse 2). Have you ever felt free enough with God to question a situation in your life that didn't make sense to you? What was the outcome?

2. Do you have a favorite psalm that helps you express yourself to God? What about it helps you in your prayer?

3. Have you ever been angry with the Lord? If so, were you able to tell him how you felt?

4. What are some reasons we might hesitate sharing our true feelings with God? How can the psalms help us to overcome any obstacles we might face?

5. How can sharing our burdens with God and expressing our true feelings with him bring us to a place of trust and acceptance? Has this ever happened for you?

Before the Next Session . . .

Below are some suggestions for using the psalms to express your feelings to the Lord. Don't feel compelled to do all of them; choose one or two that seem right for you.

1. Try to find a day or evening for a longer period of time for prayer this week. Bring a journal or some paper and write a letter to God. Give yourself permission to express any or all feelings you are experiencing—whether joy and thanksgiving, or doubt, or grief about a loss in your life, or sorrow for a pattern of sin. Tell the Lord what's on your mind. Then lift the letter to him and ask him to help you trust in his goodness and mercy. Ask him to help you work through your feelings. End your time of prayer with a psalm of praise and thanksgiving, such as Psalm 34 or 138.

2. Psalm 51 is a beautiful psalm of repentance, said to have been written by David after the prophet Nathan confronted him about his affair with Bathsheba and the murder of her husband, Uriah (2 Samuel 12). Some people pray it every day after examining their conscience. It is also the perfect prayer when preparing

for Confession. Ask the Holy Spirit to shed light on how you might be falling into sin. Then pray this psalm of repentance and ask the Lord for the grace to not fall prey to those sins in the future. Make it a point to go to Confession soon if you haven't been for awhile.

3. Verses of the psalms have traditionally been used as "aspirations," or short prayers, throughout the day. For example, "O God, come to my assistance. O Lord, make haste to help me" comes from an older translation of Psalm 70:2 and is prayed at the beginning of the Liturgy of the Hours, but we can pray it at any time we need God's help. Other verses from the psalms can express our hope in God, such as Psalm 27:1: "The LORD is my light and my salvation; / whom should I fear?" As you pray the psalms this week, find short verses that you can memorize and pray throughout the day.

FIVE

Timeless Ways to Pray with Scripture

Matthew 14:22-33

22Then he made the disciples get into the boat and precede him to the other side, while he dismissed the crowds. 23After doing so, he went up on the mountain by himself to pray. When it was evening he was there alone. 24Meanwhile the boat, already a few miles offshore, was being tossed about by the waves, for the wind was against it. 25During the fourth watch of the night, he came toward them, walking on the sea. 26When the disciples saw him walking on the sea they were terrified. "It is a ghost," they said, and they cried out in fear. 27At once Jesus spoke to them, "Take courage, it is I; do not be afraid." 28Peter said to him in reply, "Lord, if it is you, command me to come to you on the water." 29He said, "Come." Peter got out of the boat and began to walk on the water toward Jesus. 30But when he saw how strong the wind was he became frightened; and, beginning to sink, he cried out, "Lord, save me!" 31Immediately Jesus stretched out his hand and caught him, and said to him, "O you of little faith, why did you doubt?" 32After they got into the boat, the wind died down. 33Those who were in the boat did him homage, saying, "Truly, you are the Son of God."

Scripture is the inspired word of God. Through it we encounter the Lord and allow him to speak to us. But how do we listen in a way that enables us to hear him? Fortunately, we can rely on the wisdom and experience of Christians who came before us, who have much to teach us about praying with the Scriptures.

Lectio Divina

We have the desert fathers and mothers and monks of the early centuries of Christianity to thank for *lectio divina*, or the sacred reading of Scripture. In lectio divina, we choose a passage to read, such as the Gospel reading of the day. Then we ask the Holy Spirit to be with us as we read the text slowly. We may even want to read it aloud. After reading it several times slowly, we linger on a sentence or phrase that strikes us, and then spend time meditating on it.

For example, in the passage here, we may find ourselves meditating on Jesus' words "Take courage, it is I; do not be afraid" (verse 27). Perhaps we will see Jesus before us, speaking these words to us about a particular situation we are facing that scares us. Maybe another time we might linger on "O you of little faith, why did you doubt?" (verse 31), and we will think about how doubt may be undermining our faith.

The Holy Spirit inspires and guides our prayer. As we reflect on the text, we are led to pray to the Lord about what we have discovered and how we desire him to be present in our lives. Finally, we enter a period of active silence, waiting on God to give us his word or just resting peacefully in his embrace, open to receiving his abundant love.

Ignatian Meditation

Another way to nourish our prayer life is through Ignatian meditation. In this type of prayer, taught by Ignatius of Loyola, a sixteenth-century Spanish saint, we use our imagination to "fill in" the biblical scenes. First, we collect ourselves and ask the Holy Spirit to be with us. We turn to the Lord and ask him for what we desire: to get to know the person of Jesus so that we can love him, follow him, and share our lives with him. Then we read through the passage we have chosen.

> **Be honest and tell the Lord how you feel.**

We consider the context of the passage—for example, what has led up to the event described and what follows it. Then, in our minds, we imagine the place where the scene has occurred. What does it look like? What are the sounds and smells? What is the mood of the people, and what expressions do they have on their faces? In the passage here, we could easily imagine being in a terrible storm, with the wind blowing fiercely, rain pelting our faces, and looks of fear and trepidation on the faces of those around us. Perhaps we put ourselves in place of one person in the scene—in this case, maybe Peter, or perhaps one of the other apostles who is taking it all in.

After we have imagined the scene in detail, we begin a conversation with the Lord. If something moved you about the scene, tell him, or ask him why it moved you. This could lead to insights about your own life. Perhaps God is calling you to "get out of the boat," but you are afraid you will sink and are not trusting in the Lord to rescue you. Perhaps you are doubting God's care for you. Be honest and tell the Lord how you feel. Then sit quietly and listen for his word to you. You might want to write about your experience of this meditation and/ or share it with someone.

The Lord uses Scripture not only to speak to us but so that we come to know him as a true friend. It is in this type of prayer that we can encounter God, hear his voice, and receive his love. There are many resources, online and in print, to help you learn how to pray in these ways (some are listed in the appendix in this booklet). Keep in mind, however, that it is not about following a prescribed set of steps but about allowing the Holy Spirit to guide and lead us to an encounter with Jesus and God our Father.

Questions for Reflection and Discussion

1. You may have read this passage about Jesus walking on water many times before. As you read it now, what strikes you? Do you notice anything you may have missed in the past?

2. What do you think your reaction would be if you saw Jesus walking on water and then calming the winds?

3. In what ways have you benefited from praying with Scripture over these last few weeks? Have you seen

any changes in how God is working in your life during this time?

4. What has worked best for you to stay consistent with prayer? How might you overcome any obstacles you have encountered?

5. How might keeping a prayer journal help you? What about talking regularly with a friend or mentor about how your prayer is going?

For Your Life . . .

We hope these five sessions have opened up new horizons for you in your relationship with the Lord. God has so much more for us than we can ask for or imagine. Ask for the grace to be faithful to daily prayer. Make prayer a priority in your life. Don't be surprised if there are times of dryness and struggle, times when you would rather just get up and finish a chore or play with your smartphone. Resist those temptations and stay with the Lord. You will not be disappointed!

Experiment with the methods described here for praying with the Scriptures so that you can get to know

Jesus better. The explanations provided here are necessarily brief, but you can learn more by searching online or by consulting the resources provided in the appendix.

Continue to set aside a time each day for prayer. Remember, the most important reason to pray is to allow the Lord to gaze at you with love, which can only happen when you quiet yourself and sit at his feet. Find time, if you are able, to attend a holy hour at your parish. You will enjoy the silence and the powerful presence of Jesus in the Blessed Sacrament.

Scripture passages you can use in your daily prayer are listed on page 27. You can pray these and other passages again and again—you will always discover something new. Don't forget to spend some time listening as well as talking to the Lord. Be expectant that he wants to speak to you. He will forgive you, guide you, encourage you, reassure you, and comfort you. His love and mercy know no bounds.

Our Lord wants friends he can count on—friends who will radiate his love to others, especially to the poor, the lonely, and the hurting. But we can't do that until we allow him to fill us with his own love. Take Jesus up on his offer of friendship. The rewards will last a lifetime—and into eternity.

Resources

The Word Among Us magazine offers the daily Mass readings and a meditation on one of the readings for each day. www.wau.org.

iBreviary (www.ibreviary.org/en) is an app for smartphones that offers the Liturgy of the Hours, the daily Mass readings, and a host of Catholic prayers.

Thirsting for Prayer, Jacques Philippe (New York: Sceptor Publishers, 2014).

Conversing with God in Scripture: A Contemporary Approach to Lectio Divina, Stephen J. Binz (Frederick, MD: The Word Among Us Press, 2008).

The Psalms: Gateway to Prayer, Jeanne Kun (Frederick, MD: The Word Among Us Press, 2013).

Unleashing the Power of Scripture: A Guide for Catholics, Mark Hart (Frederick, MD: The Word Among Us Press, 2017).

The Ignatian Workout: Daily Exercises for a Healthy Faith, Tim Muldoon (Chicago: Loyola Press, 2004).

"Praying with Our Imagination," Creighton University Online Ministries, http://onlineministries.creighton.edu/CollaborativeMinistry/Imagination/.

"Ignatian Prayer," IgnatianSpirituality.com, http://www.ignatianspirituality.com/ignatian-prayer/.

"Pray with Your Imagination," David L. Fleming, SJ, IgnatianSpirituality.com, http://www.ignatianspirituality.com/ignatian-prayer/the-spiritual-exercises/pray-with-your-imagination.

"What Is *Lectio Divina*," Order of the Brothers of the Most Blessed Virgin Mary of Mount Carmel, http://ocarm.org/en/content/lectio/what-lectio-divina.